The Weight Of Quiet Things

A Soft Descent into Remembering

Giovanny A Guerrero

/ BookLeaf
Publishing

India | USA | UK

Made with ❤ on the BookLeaf Publishing Platform
www.bookleafpub.in
www.bookleafpub.com

Dedication

"For those who stayed — even when I didn't know how
to ask you to.
And for the ones who left — you made room for the
endings to begin."

Preface

The Weight of Quiet Things: A Soft Descent Into
Remembering
This book was not born all at once.
It gathered — like dust in corners, like memories at the
edge of sleep. It was written between silences, in the
hours when the world was quiet enough for the truth to
surface, gently.
I didn't intend to write a book about memory. I thought I
was writing about people, places, moments — but all of
it, I've come to realize, was remembering. Not the loud,
obvious kind. The soft kind. The kind that hides in the
shape of a voice you haven't heard in years, or the way a
coat still smells like the one who left it behind.
This is a book made of fragments. Each piece carries its
own rhythm — some steady, some shaking — and none
of them are asking to be solved. They are meant to
be *felt*. You don't have to understand them all at once.
Let them sit with you. Let them echo.
This book is for anyone who has tried to hold something
that couldn't be kept — a person, a time, a version of
themselves. It's about the weight of small things: a
glance, a sentence that lingered too long, a goodbye you

never got to say out loud. These things shape us more than we know.

My hope is that this book doesn't shout at you. I hope it **whispers**. I hope it reminds you how powerful softness can be — and that even in absence, there is presence. Even in stillness, movement. Even in forgetting, the memory still hums.

Above all, I hope it brings you closer to your own relationship with words — not as something to master, but something to lean into. Words don't always need to explain. Sometimes, they just need to hold space.

Thank you for reading. Thank you for remembering with me.

Acknowledgements

To acknowledge everyone who shaped this book would
be to trace a constellation of quiet moments, shared
silences, sharp truths, and soft departures.
Each piece in this work was inspired — not in isolation,
but in relation. To people. To moments. To versions of
myself I met through others.
I want to thank those whose words, gestures, presences
(and absences) found their way into these pages.
Whether you stayed for a season or simply passed
through — you left something behind that asked to be
remembered.
Every section of this book carries a different frequency.
Some are gentle echoes of love. Some are the ghosts of
pain I needed to learn how to name. Others are layered
with laughter, conversation, stillness, or longing. All of
them came from experiences I was shaped by, and all of
them were drawn into a kind of harmonic alliance —
woven through reflection, elaboration, and rhythm.
Thank you to those who unknowingly gave me language.
And to those who taught me what couldn't be said —
only felt.
This book is not about any one person, but it is filled
with the fingerprints of many. I am grateful for every
single one of you.

And finally, to the reader: thank you for stepping into this space, for letting the quiet speak, and for honoring these fragments with your presence.

1. Movie night

Their a list of things to do
or a chance to break free
it's given every day
where clouds cover most of the sky
where busy minds only have it together
when it's all been cleared
why not go out and come back
enjoy it with no rush
like what prompted was a promise
why not break free
in three days or after 10 years
Given the chance would feel like water droplets falling
off the trees
a moment to say ghostly is the life you could have lived
shooting stars would represent a singularity
moments only for you
vivid dreams or Astro projections
where the mind can meet two souls in love
opposite points to create the connection
but define the universe in your own words

1

I could hear how you'd go on and on every day
what would it feel like?
to meet the part of you that flew every other week
or sent cute pictures of the sunsets
having a list of things my heart wouldn't ever want to let
go of it would just tear a hole in the fabric
distressed or ruined
I see the beauty in your eyes
like I could feel,see and hold
more then just moments
or a list but uniquely defined
glazed over that singular moment preserving you like art
in my gallery
at awe with your mind like a new fascination everyday
or even with the way this repetition feels so natural for
you to ease out of the way of conflict gracefully more
then just saying your shine couldn't be held down in one
day
so right after that feeling and right after you
was what felt like

Every day that I think of the night,
I feel like I remember I met you
and
the good song on repeat
I think—that when I say the way I end up singing, that's
what I live in a day

feeling like every single day

one day long

time to mess you up

That movie over and over again probably a movie.

There's only one time where you were here for a while,

but it is a kiss to love

every night

that I think of the night.

What could you remember

I remember being outside

Sitting just close to the door

No wonder I heard it's so clearly

Cause the cure was to clash intently

Like forces or ours calm

the spirit or the live

Love like it's live

It's your day we could go see a movie and be up all

night

Seeing it with you could be our thing

Gazing at the stars

Looking at a screeen

Or being enchanted by your eyes

So to often I remember I met you

2. September plays

It could have been the darkness of the possibilities or the
light in the night
but where you often find your own path is near the
things you love the most
you could wonder
you could travel
but that which brought you joy
was what was there when you lost your way
like a beacon in your life the feeling of its proximity
Feels like floods or waves crashing on the shore
waiting in the sand
or floating in the clouds
which thoughts ponder your mind ?
when your breath feels how I felt the presence of your
soul
gazing back at me or when the love mirrors?

Could you say looking in I see?
I gave this a thought
please is horrendous

but the softness of my voice
created a love deep into the connection
of what was felt was lost in between
I saw were in life there was room to heal
and found September
a month before the storm an addition to that
I could say it's a good thing
because it's need
gods of gates and rites to cleanse
seven times and then there's you
A lot to process nothing to prove
life's grateful changes
nine years ago who would have thought
September be a pregame show to celebrate life
I mean do something and dedicate a part of your life into
one month that your goals align like why it'd be so
important
given to caress your soul in deep space
says a plays of every shot missed
And where every note was.

3. Count of the days

It could have been the way I was counting on that you
were actually busy
to busy to care
to busy to worry
to busy to notice
like I wasn't counting the days I hadn't seen you
I was counting the days to the goals
all I was able to accomplish before we met
like more then just sadness in a world full of creative
love
but a step by step a kiss to kiss
a lore of your grace
Lovely guides in the air
forces of yours like miracles
appearing from thin air or alive with grace
crossings are like apparitions of late projections
wishful thinking that lures
the mind into thinking of your most precious moments

I know what it might have been

The way I felt like I was lost in time
I know allot of it cause
It was what it was able to do for me
I remember the rest being pretty
The tests on why I heard your voice
I count the moments if you'd like
The time in the car
The lovers good bye
The way you said everything is going to be okay
The trip I had on my way
The visit to see you afterwards
The next morning
If I keep going I could count the days
If I loose hope
If when you don't not call
If when you took it back
But not when it was you and I
Reasons to keep counting the days
How would I feel asking if you knew the count of
the days
If you knew what I was planing in mind

4. Passing of purpose

See you know I ain't gonna wear a mask and treat you
like a little task
Cause I know it's not a little aSssk
It's raw baby
The type of love
I can see who it is you want
Deep inside
Deeper into the mind
Digging a path
Made habits just for you
Escaping the darkness
For all the times I knew
I believe it
And build it too
See the trip take me furthEr
then wonder cues
And see I could do anything for you
The ways I dodge the men who ain't you
The women who ain't good news
It's Supports

for me and you

I made it real

Authenticity

It took me some time

And time to get through

Ooo

When they said to them selfs

I knew him back in the day

Before he had the money and car and attention that
came

But he a good dude

He charismatic

Live and love

Laugh that'll make you feel at home

Cherish this man

Writhing all the different times he kept it on

A sauce of his own

A Life so nice

Reads books with good flow

And keeps it at ease

Fellow to please

See me on the Hwy

Watching you pass like

oh okay bye

You'll seem to remember me like oh why

Mystery Girl
Ion no i thought I was her
Erase me from your thoughts
Oh the thoughts
That thought I cared
But you said I let you down
So you said I guess I don't wear the crown
I see how I'm running go in Your mind
But I'm guy who came in as I am
And I still feel the waves
But it's must be a cloudy night
The way I say it's easy

Them ideas that came
Ok
Ooooo
Well here we go
That's the message that came
After breaking in

5. Remember spirit

See I want to remember
That I've changed
All the things I got to rearrange
Cause I'm the one who really came
The hardest fit to adjust to
Could even compare
The feelings of you trying to stare down the love of my
life
It toughened me up
Just to say to you
I ain't been out of luck
Just struck out with those who was trying to compare
The game with the player
It's the same
I'm the one who said you ain't insane enough
To continue and push through
It's the year of punks
Empty words but hella inner strength
Checking in and out
Just to see who came

Who was worth the pain
Memories of those moments
That made me consider
What it was really gonna take
To feel like you can finally say
It's time to walk away
So I can say
Remember that I've changed
All the things I got to rearrange
Caused me to see
Things clearly
Feeling like oh man that shit so silly
Stressing the facts that had nothing but a hold of their
minds
And trace of their lives
Like a printer it's appalling
To see it copy something that ain't on the screen
It's technically something from a new scene
A new being
Like I've been laced with the best drugs
And the doctors are the ones who have me prescribed
Cause it's more then just a sudden change
It's an analytical thing
Your gonna get to feel this energy
Even if it's from afar on a screen
It'll be on tele
Radio coverage

Like conversions that stimulate those who wanna scream
and plead
It's not me
I'm not guilty
This isn't my game
But I do have a space where you can feel safe and secure
And I can feel sure your gonna wanna keep dosing it

Casually or not the way you emerge is almost like
watching the seasons
Knowing that if you look away the leaves might start
changing color
Or when the feelings of crossing your being feels more
then just magical
The remembrance of the spirit before love or chaos
Nights where the world glows for you in such
alignments
Forth coming is what your being was able to do for my
spirit
Why not call the spirit back in
Not forgetting to mention the attachments
Like this would be the only way you'd get to remember
what it felt like

6. Lost in transactions

If I could
I would
then I did
Looking at you
Seeing the hoops
Swap me in
Looking forward to cap
Captured
Like in a movie scene
Why would not break out the love
Just to get a taste of it again
Yeah oh oh yeah
Looks like a mirror or what you can't have
Perhaps you do or and you might just like it
The way
I see it you can
Coders wanna bounce around and say
What you think it is
Na na na
I know z but

healing even if it's the "it gotta be Chaotic "
In my way it don't belong
But I love that it's ironic
Love that it platonic
Lovers who say it all early
But I left it
Or more it left me
So confused they don't know

Maybe it was the way you might have saw the mirrored
sillily
Like what you wished for leave your gaze
Section on the tension of what was in between the loses
and the only other thing that would have been the
difference
Breaking the rules and setting fires to what you were or
would have become
Seeking or flowing
Often is what feels occult
The things you read
How it's seen on your face
Like second to sense the disapproval

7. Please check out your smile

Maybe, just maybe, you see that I was always looking for my best friend(you). It was a beautiful autumn, and its pace felt so right, like a scary thought that it could be that perfect (when we meet). But when this calm and steady heartbeat feels like warm nights and busy minds, I tend to clear my mind for a while and see myself from a distance (the ever-present thought of love in the back of my mind).

It's a confidence in the Persistent smile
The tone in your voice
The grace of your healing
Abundantly radiate
To ominously say to you how you love me
Silent instead of silenced

8. Calling me back

See I don't wanna fall victim to your ego
Have myself asking were did we go
Watching it like a regal
Im i up high or down down low
Shit you about to find out tho
Built to break repair and rebuild
You should see what I do
Tell you to watch the clues
And Be who's who
In area of a field you know I've had dominant
Like you think that experience is new
Heheh he's chew chew chew
Three is the only number you can dial
No one person there but computer playing with your
life
Train of thought through wireless communication like
you didn't know
Incentives
Like know it's not something you wanted
But with no choice is it a of which knife to lick

Kick boots and rocks

To think you can have me

And I allow this to happen again you'd see why you see

Powerful grace

Huddle of a faith

Chances is you don't even see it but your getting a taste

of what I made

A warrior

A master

Something made to break

To come back strong and show you why you shouldn't

have tried to test my faith

Like a way of life that went deep into your heart

And took the chance to pull out your soul

Bring it into the light

To see this version of you

Daum it's divine

The energy like a chance

I might let you choose to follow or lead

If you knew who stands by me

It was of pure intention the call

Even the text

Seeing what was unsent

The feeling of how often I saw the alternative

Asking as if it's what was done before

In the different world were it was never important before

or even asked
To be thought of like it's not demanded
But where to ever get it going without the fear of it
being taken down to nothing
Cause no fear comes from the amount of times you can
call me
From zero to 1
To the amount of times I'm on your agenda like an
unwritten rule
Concerning should feel like there must be a real reason
to why it's not consistent

9. You left behind

You know that I see it
How gracefully beautiful you are
From the way to talk to the way you smile
You know how I see it
The time it took from me
And what it was worth for you
The saddest things it could have ever played
Your festering mind
My desire for not falling behind
The test but ain't no one score
Teller of beats and designs
Just to settle the scores
Like you say saved on my phone
Till the moment it finally feels like enough
a change of paths
The redirection of my life
Is no sudden change
But something bamboo high
Graphics of these nice times
Always on my mind

And it's worth it every minute and every high every bye
Every line
The words you got to say to me and man
Towers in my head
But it don't break my bones
just made me sweet
Taste of the sounds
Like cravings of that which feels like is falling
And here I am again
You thinking about it to
Might just like it
When you say it
But you play it
Oh daum you made it
Like you said
Just likes a sudden picture fracture game
I know it ain't all the same
Baby girl baby boy baby lore
Homies swear
Girls always loud
And know it's not
Girls swear
Boys ain't homies
And choice is to have it done
Cause it's how I know
That I ain't ever have to make that choice
It's me

I speak I don't need a repeat

You know that I see it

There are habits that help repeat the sense of peace the mind craves and to its gain the signs that repeat when someone is observing your behavior, its clear to a path of emotional peace.

Why, where and when your actions calmed my spirit like a healthy dose of sunlight.

Driving around in your mind cruising to the melodic rhythm of your heart is soothing too but it's like an experience enhanced or different somehow every time. I've more than once said what habits are mind and what habits I found are mine.

10. Nature boy

Your brave for living the way you do
Your brave for loving even through your own
You have a kind heart and great outlook on life
But your brave for it
A soul that's felt the heart ache and pressure
And gave love in return
Never tried to feed the hate
But immediately changed my mind
With the way you love
The times you said love was a test
To see me beyond the emotions
To feel me in my depths
Even though your pain
Even with the chance to feel doubt
You gave your heart a break
Cause perfection is completion
And what your looking for is a soul that's felt and sees
the beauty in life
In each and every time you felt someone glow
When you know you have this great smile

A little more you everyday should be your slogan
And you have a great way of expressing this feeling
It's timeless
Your more then just this feeling
Your brave
Your name
Your essence
It's a beautiful song
And a harmonic tune
There be the tendencies I wish to have
The most beautiful person
Brave for loving
Brave for speaking up
Brave for pushing back
Brave in addition to all the things you do to make your
life feel like you were doing what felt like second nature
A second chance is more then enough
Cause your the type that wouldn't try
You'd do
Cause trying is only attention
And you just do it to feel like one day someone will say
Daum where were you this whole time
And they'd realize that little voice that always said your
worth it fight back keep punching keep going don't give
up
All felt like you
When you gave love in such a pure form

First to ever to say don't play
First to give me love
Your brave

11. Kissed healed demons only sign

Going back to back
Then back and forward
I feel how it would have been
to have the right words to say
Or feel my own words
Change how it is that u feel
More and more
I see the need of breaking down the barriers
And rebuild the connection
But between you and me
It's ecstatic
The flow ignited
The show of love
Bringing in a new form of another
It's a kind of means bring
Like personality traits
I don't mean to boost your self esteem
But it's something really great about you
That paired with a dream

Leaning on my shoulder
It's then that you start to feel
What my words were able to do
Completely changed
Compliments to the chef
Complicated or not
The love that feels the same
Like you know
The patients I crave
The repeated respect
The love that'll never end
You can't help but be you in a way
And it's that start of a life that felt so good
To feel your embrace
To feel it be more than just a hug
It's tough my love
The life
you and I live
He said there's magic in being friends
It's more then just hello and good bye
It's the see you later
It's The next time
The love to live by
A hope of seeing what I planted
Grown and see it's bring back seeds of its own
Happiness is seeing what it would have been
And you still choose to honor yourself

Instead of putting other people first
It's a love between me and you

12. Hold on gravel is like quicksand

Hold on hold on hold on
I wanna feel the beat
the way it feels like to feel the floor with my bare feet
Or maybe it's something more
The way I say I don't know what I stand in when I'm in
the dream of you like an auto guided meditation
Grifting on the shore or falling into the pits of sand I
wanna know
The way it's feel grinds on my toes
The differences
The things I align with while maybe even tempting
The theory in why I like to know what I'm standing in
Why the gravel is firm and compacted
And the sand flows freely almost like sinking in
Solid foundations or something fluid
Sinking into something unknown
unless by design faltered
The firm grip of why grasping
Across all the lines

Where there could be purpose
Where the thought was measured
To the degree on why emotional maturity is a key role

13. Comets

It's so wild
it's so pretty
It's so me
The flowers, your picking
Get some seeds
Plan it out
Like you know
Definitely going
Big read
Birds chirping
Living it young
Cause all that mattered
Was getting it through
You know
I know
What it means snow
The chapter gonc just say it
The love looks good
But to you it didn't really matter
I was the bestselling bet

Cause I look forward
And just act on it
And own it
The same goes for you
Feeling the tension
Always getting up in my mentions
Hesitate it for a bit
I've been feeling bad
So just give me a second
I'm trying to fix it

The story that help you gather
Who it was I lost being
Feeling shot out the sky
Back to reality
You feel my heart
Yup
Good
Hey

14. Topographical road

See I could be wrong
but I could also be right
To sit here and beg
Be here and pled
To be heard
It was a feeling that felt lost
Cause to learn
what it was
felt like losing hope
Asking what it was that I did wrong
Till I left it all behind and started all over again
Nothing to break
And Everything I could be
Seeing it fall apart to make room for me
Seeing it align
to help me become
the best version of me
And seeing you in the eyes of a different life
Help me realize how simple it would have been
To ask me if everything was okay

To check up and see

What it was going on

So I could be wrong

But I could also be right

To see you and be

The ultimate person

The one in your mind

Seeing you win

Not Being like the rest

Trails but I'm the best

Healing the lows and reaching the highs

And just saying good bye

So you can say hello

To this new version of me

Keep it under control

Your mind has been on such a good ride

Healing at just the right time

Clarity of the feeling is so divine

Maybe it more then just time

I think you'd love it

If only you just try

It's a matter of realizing

The love that shined beyond the limits of time

And seeing and saying that's mine

15. Violin visions

See I could be wrong
For breaking fast
But I mean you know what I mean
When I use different words
And you feel me too
The same feeling in match
Like I speak lovers fluent asleep
Sea of the breeze
Curtain please
Ooooo
Hey
No mistake
But I know what you're saying
we're living different lives
buffalo flys
Trouble that hides
And it's other lives
that help
Them make them
You call my heart

All the time just wanna let you know
It's how I feel
I feel the glee
It's dim
But no mistake it can shine
Painful to see someone paint your most vicious terrors
But in a language that had a grip of harmony like its
legacies
pardon the pains of times where you're forced to heal
and move right on over, railing your dreamscapes to a
world of tranquility for while your heart is beating to
fast your being was inside finding the calm state of mind
slightly hearing the tone of how everything is said
for the search insights the moment it'd be found
like syphoning the vision
filtered and enhanced to decipher
the message from the soulism
forming the mind in the direction of luck
mystics and healers with sage in the air
that derives with flow and change
that it not be to reproachful but tranquil and it inspire
That the need for the serene to flourish
be shown like grace in a moment to feel the art

16. Sing like this to me because

See im a temperature control gage
Even at an old age
I can crash out
Fill up a whole page
Just here to adjust your dose of sage
Pleasure to never pled
Never mind the pain
Just realized it'll all come together
When I focus on the fourth phase
New and up and coming
But it ain't poor play
But feeling of finally feeling amazed
Freed from th role
No dummy tuck and roll
Scuttle in the line of those rhymes with lie management
and munipulations
Keeping the game
But never keeping the peace
The shoes of a guy

And knew where he was placed to seat
So it the studies of this day
And games of different plays
To adjust and be able to say
I knew and know
It's something more

So Much More
So much more

Then just trauma
Or comebacks
But you know I could come back
And do this back to back
A good time original line
A feeling of mine
To see and know what I do
When I get to open that door
Or open speech to speechless homes
Addressing people with grace
Or dignity
To say it time for you to gain control
And change the rules to the game
It isn't fair that your in such pain
And I ain't doing for you
But for ya mamas
Cause they deserve

Someone more sane
To live and cherish you with all the gains

17. Dreams of you

It's an irresistible charm
But that's when it gets you
Like being pulled in with no escape
Then things you buys to make you feel okay
And the things that come in to replace
The things l wish I never had a chance to but here we go
Love and hate it
But I could never betray it
The love deep inside
Instrumental
Love and its ties
Hate and its fires
I see it rise then become like water to me
Fluid in a drean
Come and come
Like I'm waiting for you to see where I've been
And what it feels like to unlock my eyes
To all the things and all of the plays
It's like watching a movie production program
Where this life is what I know

And I'm trying to hope
And build from space
I'm safe in
You see the feng shui of it
like I'm on it or no
I know what you'd like of course
I'm on the direction of it
Like fine dining on a six course meal
Check it cause I'm ready to go
I've pull it in with me and you
And there we go
Getting and going
No problems ahead
I've made sure I'm made consistency of it
The way it express my love
And the way you might even hate it
But I could never betray it
It's an irresistible charm
The deep hate it's blocking you from it
Even when I know it
I might just play it over and over
Just for you and me

18. Familiarize your ears

See I won't be crushed by it
I know what you mean
I know what it is
You want freedom on a level playing actions I see it how
you can be protected
The mean of assistance
Like a credible source
I checked more then once it's how level the score
Even if you don't want me to say it
I'm setting up not speaking up
Cause it's getting loud
I hear them scream
With out a second to speak
I tried it best be the love
But it's crashed out rebels or man who thrown back
more then a pebble
I sweety thence forward calm to the mind
The way I see it
I don't let it fall to behind
But why or why

Oh why
Mountain moving fast but
I need to see it change
in the places that would most bettter the quality of life
I see it can be done
There is if so
Chance to get built
The international feel
If you can see me
You gonna have to know
That now your in it
It's wild isn't it
Being in a society
Where negative thoughts can really control how you feel
What you do
How you feel about others
What a wild thing it is to think
Savage almost
Being in a feeling of red your whole life
And all you see is the rainbow
Being a being of insatiable freedom
Woah might have said it to loudly
I dare you to experience it
The echoes of mine
Like the mind of a young me
Shooting lasers out of my eyes from being angry
Shut up your to loud

Sit down take you place in line
Dragged across the floor
Are the words that would ever try to hold me on a path I
did not choose
Rules you didn't want
Limitation like shit
Will I finally scream my truth
Like trusting I have no fear
Watch your mouth
Cause ain't it wild
To think you can feel just how I feel
I'm becoming the more authentic everyday version of
myself everyday
And man ain't it wild
To see the mirror
And see it was still young me
Looking back at me
F*ck yes.
Speaking a language that broke cyphers
Interesting kid
Showing me where all my dreams hide tangible to the
mind
So true
But ain't it wild
What a influence it is that you let yourselves be fed
I guess it's not to different
Besides the fact of my happy dance

No poison cooler then me
if where you find true happiness
Ain't nothing to not say it
Cause ain't it while
Doing things so other can do it too
Or seeing which and every way you got to be a person
discovering the veil
Mesmerized by smiles and energetic flow
Step by step
Closing doors and opening new ones
Ending chapters and pushing through
New plains of existence
You can call it euphoric
The way that life shows you that you have control over
what you accept
Over time accomplishing something that broke barriers
and built bridges
In a whole where the past gave us The chance to make a
change beyond their belief
And in each and every day you think about it
Ain't it wild

19. First night

See, I could picture the love,
but I love you more than that.
I could picture what it took for me to feel like you'd see
the love of my life hear these words,
but I love you more than the words could ever express.
Like, is that you?
Remember the way I kissed your lips?
Why it felt like a moment
, in a way it felt like something more?
And, well, to be honest, I could picture the love,
but I love you more than just that.
Like finding each part of you in me, in time.
Trying to see you want to spend time with me in the
most loving ways,
but I love you more than any moment can show.
I picture the beach, the hiking trails, and the places we
had ever been.
But to be honest, there's so much more to a sweet, caring
soul—
and I love you more than any of those places.

There's the way you feel, the aura of how often you felt
like a reminder, but really dove deep.
You felt like more than moments saved on my phone.
You were the picture in a movie that I most wanted to
life.
The feeling of seeing the things that made you love,
and to say I still say you're the love of my life,
I love you more than just the way I feel, but the way I
felt.
It's what I because cause I cared too much.
I was the feeling that most people would love to feel—
and I love you more than they could ever imagine.
To see that the senses came alive when you walked in a
crowd,
like almost an eclipse.
Seeing you shine was like a beautiful picture,
a quick film, a short time only, like a trailer that would
have been the most romantic event.
And till the day you say "I do," and even after,
I'd be the guy.
The one who says how beautiful you are.
The one who sees that the best part of my day is you.
You could ask me how often,
and you'd know I'd respond.
But the notes and memories I carry in my heart are those
of a devoted love.
Like, would it feel like a little more like you if I'd just say

your name?
But to say you're the love of my life, and the love in my
life—
I love you more than I could ever express.
So, I could picture the love,
but I love you more.
I could picture the movies,
but I love you more than any story could tell.
I could sense the way it was more than just a memorable
person,
but I love you more than anyone else.

Seeing the way we spend our days,
the way it felt like always searching for each other,
I could be the voice, but I could also be the hand on your
shoulder, saying, "I know it'll all be okay."
That even after the sun has gone down, and the moon is
shining our way,
you feel me say, "Could I stay a little bit longer?"
Cause to love you, you'd see my heart,
and I love you more than I can say.

Where would it be—the heart of a soul that lived and
loved art like a dream or a song—to see how often the
memories were like being that which it wished to be?
And no matter what, I love you more than that.

20. The day before the headache

And I see the habits forming
And I see my life changing
And What couldve ever happened
Lovely life
Or something comfortable
To be able to rise or drown and it be nice
To know when it was this happened
Easy to sign away your right
But to fight is a passion
And feels fright are just lonely sights
A changing light
Ready to go
Ready for a change
The chance comes everyday
In it for the report back
Suddenly the saddled is up
And I'm feeling the wind
Rising sun
Gleaming sight

Rolling right into a wall

But I stand tall

Big brother is always on

Live a love story that's always right

Right by your side

Or something else

Taller than me

Beamed up like a light

Idea of me

Mine the love you crave

Insight of yours has a heart falling in love

Memories are made

Then new ones came

In and Now

There is - was the solution

You ever keep me

Break me or something else

I'm out here on another channel

Tuning in

Fixing the lines for content connection to be made

The set of mine

Would be perfectly fine

Asking for much more

Like yeah heallo yeah I'm tapped in

Ready to play

Record

rushed out the door isn't what I felt but an estimated

time frame for the perfect pickup
exclusively leaving it at the door
or calling it open door kisses
rules to the sight of signs to say if signs say so
but oh my do the winds blow when fires roll in
deep breaths into observing you

21. Replace the repetition with something better

It's moments
The smiles that come without force
Like conversations that just flower with ease like almost
showing confidence
if to say that I remember the feeling
Like what I miss the most
I grasp the chance to as much as i can
If not to say that it was the best
it was the greatest feeling
Being there with a group of people I called friends
Connections so deep like feeling how much they actually
care and wanted the best
If when I see you it's like a hug that never felt anything
ever got close
It's just more then saying it's your
"but a series of events that gathered the crowd "
A person
A smile
An entertaining game we played with each other like

wanting to know what it was we liked the most Seeing
you search the parts of my mind just to giggle at how
geeky I felt when you saw the parts of me not many see
If not only to say I was fan girling
how often it was that

the things that made me happy

It's moments
The ones that most captured my love the essence of joy
Like the innocence in our kiss
the touch of our hearts softly rocking us to sleep
And to me it was more then just moments
It was how often I wanted to be there with you
Seeing you smile
Seeing you
Just like a glowing heart that to me was like a star I put
in my pocket
Just to save you for another moment
A moment that would be just for us
A moment that to me would be the love like one only we
had with each other
A moment that became the connection
Of how often we thought of each other.